DOUBLE TROUBLE
With
DICK and JANE

D1568852

Written by Roseann Hotz Woodka, PhD

Illustrated by Elena Bogatireva

Roseann Hotz Woodka
2021

Double Trouble with Dick and Jane is the second of three children's books depicting the story of their lives.

As in *Precious Moments with Dick and Jane*, *Double Trouble* consists of vignettes divided into five sections: Mommy, Grandma's House, The Ball, Jane, and Dick. Each of the vignettes describes the antics of these two mischievous "dogettes."

No longer puppies but not quite adult dogs, I made up the term "dogettes." As you will see in this book, Dick and Jane look like mature dogs but behave like playful puppies.

Just like human children, Dick and Jane love to be loved and love to give love. When dogs are in the house, there is enough love for everyone.

The values on the last page: safety, cooperation, obedience, helpfulness, learning, fun, and curiosity are values I hope children and adults will incorporate into their daily lives.

Enjoy reading the second stage of life with Dick and Jane.

Roseann

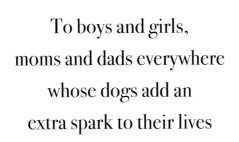

To boys and girls,
moms and dads everywhere
whose dogs add an
extra spark to their lives

"and so our story continues..."

We were puppies for a l-o-o-o-ng time. Mommy said there were two of us
so we were double cute, double sweet, and double TROUBLE!

We liked to chew on Mommy's fingers. Sometimes she would say "ouch." We didn't want to hurt her so we chewed on the legs of a kitchen stool. The only problem was it was the stool her grandpa made for her when she was a little girl. "Oops!"

We felt bad about that so we switched to a rug in the dining room. I guess that wasn't a good idea, either.

Agility

When we were about 6 months old, Mommy took us to doggy obedience school. It didn't sound like much fun to us. We were supposed to learn tricks, to share our toys, and obey Mommy.

The teacher said school was really for Mommy. The teacher fooled us. When graduation day came, we were the ones who had to wear those silly hats...not Mommy.

5

In the Spring, we liked to help Mommy by digging holes for her so she could plant flowers. We had fun digging in the dirt. Mommy said she liked to dig in the dirt, too.

We REALLY liked playing in the mud after she watered the flowers. Mommy wasn't always happy with us at that point. She called us "dirty double trouble."

One time when we had mud all over us, Jane hid so Mommy wouldn't give her a bath. It didn't work. Mommy spotted her behind the pretty plants and gave her a bath anyway.

Mommy's version of a bath was putting us in the kitchen sink with soap and water. We didn't like it as much as we liked that very first bath at the nice lady's house.

In December, Mommy had friends over for a Cotton Bowl football party. We love parties and playing games. We played tug-of-war with a stuffed football. We tugged so hard the football fell apart. We decorated the whole kitchen with pieces of cotton. We called it a "cotton ball party." We had so much fun. Mommy and her friends thought we were very funny and very mischievous.

Holidays and birthdays are really special at the office. Mommy's office friends have parties for us. They bring treats, doggie ice cream and presents. The only problem is that

Mommy dresses us up in the most embarrassing outfits. Rain coats, Santa hats and birthday hats are bad enough, but the Halloween costumes are the worst. She thinks we look cute, but we don't.

We love to visit Grandma. One Sunday Grandma and Mommy left us alone while they went to church. Grandma had all kinds of pink and purple violets in her living room. Since we love to decorate, we pushed the pots off the table and made the prettiest garden on Grandma's carpet. It had dirt, leaves and, of course, pink and purple violets. We were so proud of our talent.

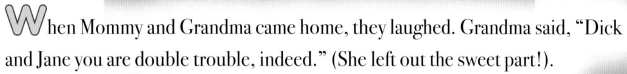

When Mommy and Grandma came home, they laughed. Grandma said, "Dick and Jane you are double trouble, indeed." (She left out the sweet part!).

One time we were supposed to be outside going potty. We decided to leave Grandma's yard and check out her neighborhood. We chased squirrels up the trees. We ran past other dogs, barking at us from inside their fences. As usual we were having fun together. The only problem was, we got lost.

A man saw us walking down the sidewalk of a busy street. He gathered us up and took us to the police station where we would be safe. The police people were really nice, but they put us in doggie jail so we wouldn't get lost again. We were kind of scared, but at least we were together.

They called our mommy and Grandma. We were really happy to see them. At first Mommy cried and hugged us tight. Then she scolded us for leaving Grandma's yard. She loves us no matter what we do.

PLAYING BALL

Playing fetch is an all-time favorite. Mommy throws the tennis ball with a "chuck it" (or it won't go very far). We run as fast as we can to get it and bring it back. Sometimes we can't find the ball so Mommy throws another one. She can't fool us, though. We want the one that says, "Dick and Jane."

We play ball in the swimming pool, too. It is a blue ball and squeaks really loud. The pool lady calls it our "magic" ball. We swim as fast as we can to get it. It doesn't matter which one of us gets it first. Like all brothers and sisters, we never fight over it. Haha!

In the winter we get lots of snow. Mommy loves snow. We do, too. Mommy makes balls out of the snow. She calls them snowballs. She throws one ball. We put our faces in the cold, wet snow to find it, but it's never there! We can't figure out where it went. Mommy laughs at us, and throws another one. (We can't find this one, either!).

JANE

At work I love to get in the trash. There are so many interesting smells and tastes in there. It's especially fun to drag the trash out into the waiting room when clients are there. They love to watch me make a mess.

One time I got into some green stuff that the mice were supposed to eat. It didn't taste that good, but I ate it anyway. I guess it makes puppies REALLY sick. That wasn't so funny.

21

Mommy rushed Dick and me to the puppy hospital. She wasn't sure which one of us ate it so the doctor made both of us throw up. Yuck! I was the only one with the green stuff. Dick was not very happy with me, but he still loves me.

Mommy calls me a "little stinker." Mommy relaxes in her favorite chair at night. Sometimes Dick gets on Mommy's lap first, and I want to be there. I just go to the door and ring the wind chimes. That means I have to go potty. Dick jumps up and runs outside. I turn around and jump in the chair. He falls for it every time!

DICK

I love it when clients bring us doggy bones. Jane eats hers right away, but I don't. I walk around the office until I find the best place to hide it. Sometimes I bury it in the cushions of the sofa. I guard it just in case Jane, or anyone else for that matter, tries to find it.

One time I forgot where I hid it. When Mommy's client sat down on the sofa, he felt something sharp on his bottom. He jumped up holding my lost bone. I was so happy he found it for me. I gave him a big kiss.

The best therapist has fur and four legs

We like to ride in the car while Mommy runs errands. One day Mommy got a whole bunch of food. Then she stopped at a store for children. She likes to shop for her grandkids. She stayed in the store way too long, however, and I got bored.

The groceries looked pretty interesting. I decided to check the bags out.
There were some really good things in there like cookies and muffins. I
decided to help myself. Yum! I left the lettuce and tomatoes alone. I know
how much Mommy likes her salads.

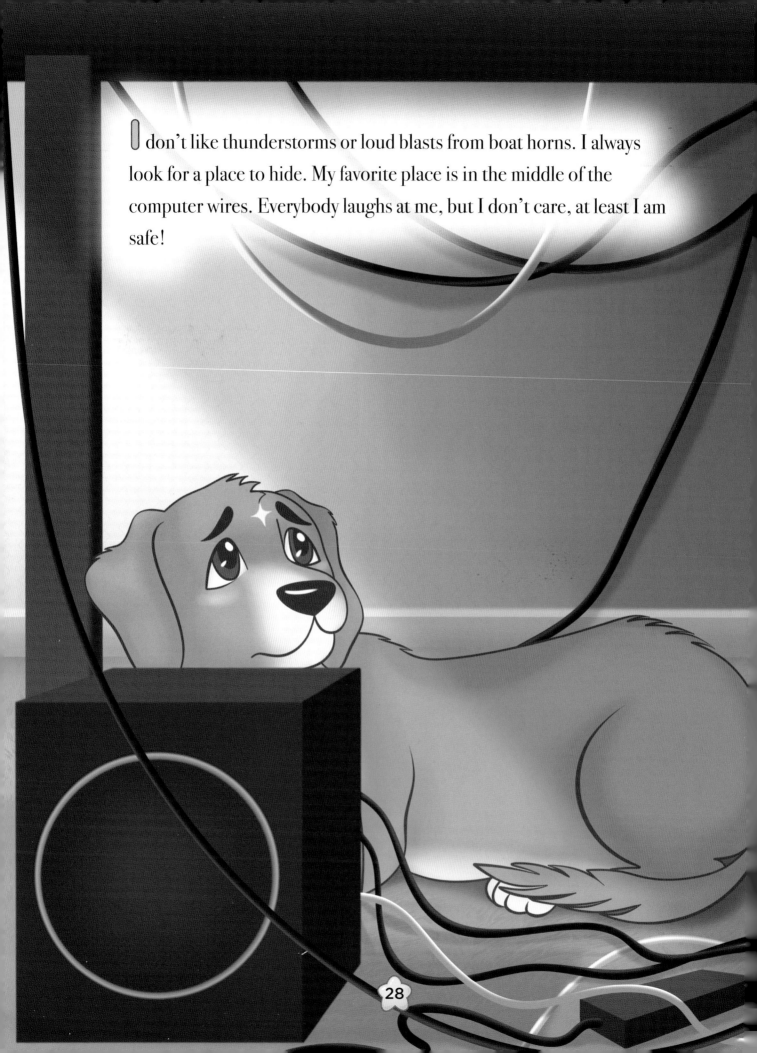

I don't like thunderstorms or loud blasts from boat horns. I always look for a place to hide. My favorite place is in the middle of the computer wires. Everybody laughs at me, but I don't care, at least I am safe!

VALUES

Mommy thinks praying is important. While most puppies "sit pretty" for their treats, we pray. There must be a God for puppies. Mommy says it's the same God that she has.

CONSCIENCE

CURIOSITY

COOPERATION

FUN

LEARNING

HELPING

OBEYING

MISCHIEF

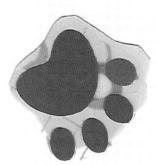

UH HO

MISCHIEF

FAMILY

FUN

1711

TOO CUTE!

SERIOUSLY

Roseann is a counseling psychologist who works in a small group practice in Elkhart, Indiana. This is the second book in the Dick and Jane series. *Precious Moments with Dick and Jane* is book one and *Senior Living with Dick and Jane* is book three. The books were inspired after many comments were made by clients who love the real Dick and Jane and have benefited from their presence. Roseann has two children and four grandchildren who witness the antics of Dick and Jane. All of them provide love and laughter on a daily basis.

Elena has a passion for illustrating picture books for children. Her illustrations capture the eyes of children and adults alike. Elena uses her gift of art in designing business cards, postcards, posters, banners, and other creative products. She incorporates art in her free time in the form of chalk painting and CG illustrations.

Look for the other two books in the Dick and Jane series.

Precious Moments with Dick and Jane.

Senior Living with Dick and Jane

For more children's books visit our web site

www.marianapublishing.com

Find us on:

 @LlcMariana | *@marianapublishing* | *@marianapublishing*

A special thanks to Roger Carlson, who coordinated the process of making this book a reality. He is tried and true and very patient. Thank You, Roger. - Roseann

ISBN: 978-1-64510-034-8 (Hardback)
ISBN: 978-1-64510-033-1 (Hardback with Sleeve)
ISBN: 978-1-64510-055-3 (Amazon)
ISBN: 978-1-64510-032-4 (Print on Demand)

First Published in 2020
Printed in the USA